D1586775

CGP has the KS2 English SATS sorted!

This superb CGP book is chock-full of practice for the KS2 English SATS, and it's totally up-to-date for the tests in 2017 and beyond!

It explains all the key English topics using crystal-clear examples, making it perfect for pupils working at or towards the Expected Standard.

We've also included plenty of practice questions to test them on what they've learned — with answers included to make marking a breeze!

CGP — still the best! ☺

Our sole aim here at CGP is to produce the highest quality books — carefully written, immaculately presented and dangerously close to being funny.

Then we work our socks off to get them out to you — at the cheapest possible prices.

Contents

Section Four — Punctuation

Section Five — Vocabulary

Section Six — Spelling

Published by CGP

From original material by Richard Parsons

Editors:
Chloe Anderson, Izzy Bowen, Emma Cleasby, Emma Crighton, Joanna Daniels, Jack Perry, Rebecca Tate

With thanks to Matt Topping and Alison Griffin for the proofreading.
With thanks to Jan Greenway for the copyright research.

Thumb illustration used throughout the book © iStock.com.

ISBN: 978 1 78294 677 9

Printed by Elanders Ltd, Newcastle upon Tyne.
Clipart from Corel®

1

About This Book

This Book has All the Key Topics for KS2

At the end of Year 6, you'll be tested on all the reading, grammar, punctuation and spelling you've learnt during Key Stage 2.

This book covers the <u>key topics</u> you might be tested on.

> This book covers the key <u>Learning Objectives</u> for <u>Key Stage 2</u> of the <u>National Curriculum</u>.

There are Practice Questions for Each Section

At the end of each section there are <u>practice questions</u>. You can see what you know and what you don't know.

There's a <u>matching Question Book</u>. It's got questions on all the topics and it also has some practice tests.

I love to practise.
I love to practise.

There are Learning Objectives on All Topics

Learning objectives say <u>what you should be able to do</u>.
Use the <u>tick circles</u> to show how <u>confident</u> you feel.

Tick here if you think you need <u>a bit more practice</u>.

If you're really <u>struggling</u>, tick here.

Tick this circle if you can do <u>everything</u> on the page.

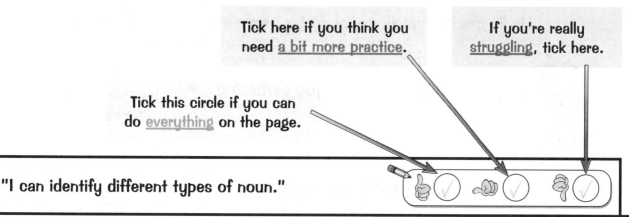

"I can identify different types of noun."

Word Meaning

Some Questions Ask What Words Mean

1) You might be asked to explain what a word from the text means.

> As he walked through the cave, the gnome heard a muffled cry from inside his sack.

If you were asked to explain the word 'muffled', you could write that it means the sound isn't clear.

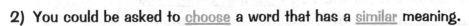

2) You could be asked to choose a word that has a similar meaning.

EXAMPLE: Which is closest in meaning to the word 'thundered' in the sentence below?

Francis thundered into the house and slumped on the sofa.

charged ✓   strolled ☐   shuffled ☐   tiptoed ☐

The Rest of the Sentence Might Help You

1) If you're not sure about the meaning of a word, use the sentence that the word is in to give you a clue.

EXAMPLE: What does the word 'reluctantly' mean in the sentence below?

> The ostrich reluctantly sat next to the robot, but fled as soon as she could.

This bit tells you that the ostrich didn't want to sit next to the robot.

2) Some words can mean different things in different sentences, so you'll need to look at the rest of the sentence to work out what they mean.

Hadia drank from the cool spring.

In this sentence, Hadia is drinking, so the spring is a source of water.

In the spring, I enjoy gardening.

Here, someone is gardening, so you can guess that spring is a season.

"I can understand and explain the meaning of words."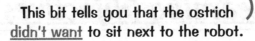

Retrieving Information

You Might Just Need to Find Information

1) Some questions just want you to find information in the text.

   EXAMPLE:

   > What happened to the postman on his way home?

   This question just needs a short, simple answer.

2) Sometimes the answers might be hard to find in the text. Scan through the text looking for words from the question. This should help you find the information.

3) Some questions will ask you to give more than one answer.

   EXAMPLES:

   > Give two reasons why Priti was angry.

   > What three things does this tell you about helicopter rides?

   Make sure you write the correct number of things. If you don't, you won't get the marks.

4) Make sure you get your answer from the text.
   Don't be tempted to answer questions using your own knowledge.

You Might be Asked a True or False Question

You might have to decide if a statement is true or false based on what you've read in the text. All the information you need will be in the text — you just have to find it.

EXAMPLE: Read each sentence and tick one box to show whether it is true or false.

	True	False
Each giraffe's pattern of spots is unique.	☐	☐
Giraffes are a popular attraction at the zoo.	☐	☐

For this type of question, make sure you only tick one box per row.

"I can retrieve and record information and identify key details from the text."

Summarising

You Might Have to Summarise

1) <u>Summary</u> questions ask about information that's <u>spread</u> across <u>different paragraphs</u>.

2) You might have to say what the <u>main message</u> of a text is, say what a <u>character</u> is <u>like</u> or answer questions where the information isn't all in <u>one</u> place.

EXAMPLE: What is the main idea of the section on birds?

This question is asking you what the <u>whole section</u> is about.

> As larger and larger areas of woodland are cut down to make way for new housing developments, birds are <u>losing their habitats</u>. It is <u>vital</u> that we work to <u>protect</u> these creatures for future generations.
>
> To <u>defend the safety</u> of these wonderful creatures, we must <u>create safe nesting spaces</u> in our gardens and continue to <u>fight</u> against those who wish to <u>destroy</u> the birds' natural habitats.

Look for any <u>repeated ideas</u> in the section — these can usually help you <u>work out</u> what the <u>main message</u> is.

The <u>text</u> talks about the <u>threat</u> to birds and the fact that they need to be <u>protected</u>.

The <u>main idea</u> is that we should make sure birds are <u>protected</u>.

Writing About Characters Can Be Tricky

1) You could be asked about a <u>character</u> — what they're <u>like</u> or how they <u>behave</u>.

2) <u>Read</u> the text and look for <u>clues</u> about that character.

3) Think about how they <u>react</u> to <u>situations</u> or how they <u>treat others</u>.

EXAMPLE:

What is the best word to describe Alan's character?

brave ✓   thoughtful ☐   humble ☐   irritable ☐

The first sentence suggests he's <u>brave</u> but <u>not thoughtful</u>.

<u>Without thinking</u>, Alan walked to the end of the diving board and <u>launched himself into the icy water</u>. He drew himself out of the swimming pool, <u>smiled</u> and then <u>gloated</u> at the other swimmers.

He smiles, so he doesn't seem <u>irritable</u>. Gloating suggests that he's <u>not humble</u>.

"I can summarise main ideas from more than one paragraph."

Making Inferences

Inferring Means Working Something Out

1) Sometimes writers <u>don't say</u> what they <u>mean</u> clearly. Instead they <u>suggest</u> something, and you have to <u>read between the lines</u> to work out the <u>meaning</u>.

2) For example, you might be asked to decide <u>how</u> someone is <u>feeling</u>.

> **EXAMPLE:** What <u>kind of mood</u> do you think Carla is in?
>
> 'Yes, it's been a really great day', <u>groaned</u> Carla.
>
> From what Carla <u>says</u>, you'd think she was feeling quite <u>happy</u>...
>
> ... but the word '<u>groaned</u>' suggests that she's actually <u>unhappy</u>.

3) You might need to <u>back up</u> your answer with <u>evidence</u>. Use <u>details</u> from the text or <u>quotations</u> (the actual words from the text) to say <u>why</u> you think you're right.

> **EXAMPLE:** How does this <u>make the reader feel</u> about the rocket's journey?
>
> The rocket swerved its way around <u>dangerous</u> asteroids, the roar of the engine powering it forward. Everyone held their breath in <u>anticipation</u>, but finally the rocket reached Planet Mop.

Words like '<u>dangerous</u>' and '<u>anticipation</u>' make you feel <u>scared</u> about the rocket's journey.

Remember to put any quotations in speech marks.

You Need to Know About Facts and Opinions

You might need to say whether something is a <u>fact</u> or an <u>opinion</u>.

If a statement is <u>supported</u> by figures or <u>evidence</u>, you can be pretty sure that it's a fact.

Ants can lift more than their weight.

This sentence can be <u>backed up</u> with <u>evidence</u>. It's a <u>fact</u>.

When someone says what they <u>think</u> about something, it's an <u>opinion</u>.

Eagles are the best birds.

This sentence tells you what someone <u>thinks</u>. It can't be <u>proved</u> with evidence. It's an <u>opinion</u>.

"I can make inferences and justify them with evidence from the text."

What Happens Next?

You Might Have to Make a Prediction

1) You could be asked to <u>predict</u> what will happen next in a text based on <u>what you've read</u>.

2) Often you'll need to explain <u>why</u> you think it is going to happen.

> **EXAMPLE:** What do you think will happen to the rooster at the dance competition?

3) <u>Before</u> you write down your answer, ask yourself these <u>questions</u>:

① What is <u>currently happening</u> at the <u>end</u> of the text?

② What is the overall <u>feeling</u>? Are the characters happy? Are they in danger?

③ What do you think is <u>likely</u> to happen next?

Your Prediction Must be Based on the Text

Make sure your prediction is <u>backed up</u> by the text — <u>don't</u> just make up anything.

> **EXAMPLE:** Do you think Freddie will visit his uncle's house again?

<u>At first</u>, Freddie seems <u>scared</u> of his uncle.

But it turns out that he's <u>kind</u> and Freddie is <u>excited</u> about the <u>sweets</u>.

Freddie <u>waited nervously</u> outside the large, <u>imposing</u> house. He'd never met Uncle George, and Freddie's dad always <u>sounded a little afraid</u> whenever he spoke about him. To his relief, his uncle opened the door <u>with a smile</u> on his face and <u>greeted Freddie warmly</u>. Freddie followed him into a comfortable-looking living room and his <u>eyes lit up</u> when he saw a big bowl of <u>his favourite sweets</u> sitting on the table. He rushed over, but then his uncle's dog, who was lying next to it, began to <u>growl menacingly</u>. For the rest of the visit, Freddie sat <u>glued to his chair</u>, trying not to look longingly at the sweets he <u>couldn't get to</u>.

In the end he seems <u>very scared</u> of his uncle's <u>dog</u>.

You could say he <u>won't go back</u> because he's scared of the dog. You could also argue that he <u>will go back</u> because he likes his uncle. You can choose <u>either</u>, as long as there are <u>reasons</u> in the text to support your answer.

"I can predict what will happen next based on information in the text."

Structure

Some Questions Ask About Structure

1) Structure questions are about how the information in a text fits together.

2) You could be asked to find the point in a text where something important happens. This could be the point where a person's feelings suddenly change or when the story swaps between locations.

EXAMPLE:

Find and copy a phrase which shows when the atmosphere changes.

Glancing behind him, Joshua could see nothing in the pitch darkness. He quickened his pace, his ears straining to catch the footsteps of his pursuer. Trying not to panic, he forced himself through a thick hedge and stumbled onto the pavement of a country lane. His breath came in gasps as he broke into a run. Suddenly, a car's bright headlights lit up the path. Joshua looked behind him and was flooded with relief. A small, shaggy horse trotted up and nuzzled his chest with its long, damp nose. Laughing, Joshua stroked it.

The text starts off sounding very scary...

... but when Joshua realises what's chasing him, the atmosphere changes to become more lighthearted.

You Might Need to Put Things in Order

1) Some questions might ask you to put events in the right order.

2) Read through the text carefully, looking for each event.

3) If you're allowed to, mark each event on the paper.

4) Then fill in the answers in the right order.

Different Bits of the Text do Different Things

You might have to say what function part of a story has — what it does in the text.

The wind whistled through the spindly trees.	My sister isn't a kind person.	The ghost chased the terrified cat.	Four years ago, there had been an accident.	She would never ignore him again.
Description or setting	Character description	Action	Background or past events	Moral or lesson

"I can explain how different parts of texts are related and describe the function of part of a text."

Choice of Language

Some Questions Focus on Language

1) The language in a text has usually been chosen for a reason.

2) Make sure you can find words which describe things in a certain way.

EXAMPLE:

Find and copy four words or phrases from the text that make the national park seem exciting.

Look for words that mean the same as 'exciting'.

There might be lots of answers to choose from, but you only need to give the number you're asked for.

Aberbeck National Park is a beautiful paradise, but also an electrifying playground for kids and adults alike! Go for a thrilling cycle along the valley floor and stare at the imposing peaks that surround you. Take a drive up winding mountain passes and look down sheer cliffs from one of the many viewing points — the drops will take your breath away. Scale down the cliffs on an exhilarating abseiling adventure, or you could even go for a heart-stopping rafting trip down the Timna River.

Language Can Tell You What Things are Like

1) You might need to explain what a word or phrase from the text tells you.

2) Think about the overall impression the text gives you and how different words and phrases make you feel about what's being described.

EXAMPLE:

What does this paragraph tell you about the kitchen?

Mrs Devani Misra ruled the restaurant kitchen. It was a whirl of activity from early morning until late at night. Waiters and chefs danced around each other — it was a miracle they never collided. Ovens roared, pans clattered, doors banged, voices gabbled, orders were barked... but out of all this came the delicious and delicate food that Devani was famous for.

The phrases in blue suggest that the kitchen is busy and full of people moving around.

The words in green suggest that the kitchen is noisy.

"I can identify how language can affect meaning."

Comparing

Some Questions Ask How Things Compare

1) You might get a question that asks you to compare how two things are <u>similar</u> or <u>different</u>.

2) Look at the <u>information</u> that is given about both things to decide on your answer.

EXAMPLE: According to the text, how are Paris and New York similar?

Paris and New York are on <u>opposite sides</u> of the Atlantic Ocean. They have <u>different cultures</u>, and their inhabitants speak <u>different languages</u>. However, they <u>share</u> the distinction of being their country's largest city and they were <u>both</u> founded on the banks of large rivers. The <u>two</u> cities have also been the setting of many popular films over the years.

This bit tells you how the two cities are <u>different</u>.

Look out for words that tell you what things have <u>in common</u>. Paris and New York are both the <u>largest</u> city in their country, and they're both on large <u>rivers</u>.

3) If the question asks for a <u>certain number</u> of similarities or differences, make sure that's the number you <u>write</u>. Otherwise you'll <u>miss out</u> on <u>marks</u>...

You Could be Asked How Things Change

1) You might also be asked how something <u>changes</u>, for example a character's mood.

2) Look at the <u>beginning</u> and <u>end</u> of the bit you're asked about, and write about any <u>differences</u> between the two.

EXAMPLE:

How does Jemma's opinion of Georgie change during the basketball game?

Write about how Jemma <u>feels</u> about Georgie at the <u>beginning</u> of the game...

... then write about how she feels about her at the <u>end</u> of the game.

"I can make comparisons within texts."

Practice Questions — Story

Read this extract from a story, then answer the questions below.

The Direction Dilemma

"Right, we'd better get going," announced Richard, swiftly draining his coffee cup and pushing back his cheap plastic chair. Beth and Ryan followed him as he marched purposefully out of the cafe.

Outside, Richard carefully extracted a map from his rucksack and spread it flat on a table. Beth and Ryan stood behind him, peering over his shoulder.

"So, we've walked here," he explained, trailing his finger along a dotted line that represented a footpath. "Now we're going to head out this way." He gestured again at the map, eventually resting his finger on a point labelled 'Woodland Cabins'.

"Richard," Ryan interrupted, "I think we should take the route that we planned. We said we'd go north after the cafe, not north-west."

"This way is better," said Richard bluntly. "We'll get to the cabin earlier and the route will be much more scenic."

Beth and Ryan exchanged a concerned look, but didn't argue. There wasn't any point — Richard would never listen. He stowed the map in his bag and set off, holding his compass. The others followed reluctantly.

Before long, they reached a footpath that carried them higher and higher over a lonely stretch of moor. The landscape looked like a painting; they could see for miles over the heather-covered hills, and in the distance there were mountain peaks sprinkled with a dusting of snow. The midday sun shone brilliantly down on them.

They walked for a few more hours, passing forests, lakes and mountains. Richard confidently led the way and the others trailed a few metres behind, still annoyed with their self-appointed leader but chatting happily among themselves.

Eventually, the sun began to set and darkness drew in, bringing with it an unwelcome chill that made Beth feel even more anxious than when they'd set off. She was about to call ahead to Richard when she saw him stop abruptly. He pulled out his map again and knelt on the ground, flattening the paper onto the grass. He paused for a moment, then jumped back to his feet.

Practice Questions — Story

"Excellent. The cabins should be just at the bottom of this hill," he said proudly.

Beth and Ryan both breathed a sigh of relief — they had begun to wonder if Richard knew where he was going.

But when they finally reached the bottom of the hill, they stopped dead in their tracks. Opposite them was a cafe — the same cafe they had visited earlier that day. The sign above the door was shrouded in darkness, so another nocturnal passer-by would have no idea of the purpose of the building. And the low light had distorted the door and windows — now it looked like a laughing, mocking face. But from the bird table outside to the three chimneys on its roof, they knew that this was the cafe they had visited just hours before. Beth and Ryan looked accusingly at Richard, who stared blankly at the cafe, his mouth open.

"But... They should be here," he said quietly, holding the map out in front of him. "I followed the map precisely..."

"Obviously not," Beth snarled, snatching it out of his hands.

"Where are we going to sleep?" Ryan said, panic rising in his voice.

"There's nowhere to stay for miles around here," Beth explained, examining the map. "We can't carry on walking — it's too dark."

Ryan sat down at the side of the road, exhausted. No one spoke for a while.

Finally, Beth broke the silence. "Well, we've got a cold night ahead of us then."

1   **Circle** the correct option to complete the sentence below.

At the beginning of the text, Richard finishes his coffee ....

quickly   slowly   carefully   noisily

2   *... Richard carefully extracted a map from his rucksack*
     Which word most closely matches the meaning of the word *extracted*?

Tick **one** box.

used   ☐

unclipped   ☐

removed   ☐

presented   ☐

Practice Questions — Story

3   Why did Richard want to take a different route to the one they had planned?
Tick **two** boxes.

Ryan told him to. ☐   It had a footpath. ☐

It was faster. ☐   It was prettier. ☐

It went past a cafe. ☐

4   Beth and Ryan were concerned about taking Richard's route.
Why didn't they tell him this?

....

....

5   Look at the paragraph beginning: *Before long, they reached a footpath...*
Why were they able to see for miles over the hills?

....

....

6   *...sprinkled with a dusting of snow.*
What does this tell you about the snow?

....

7   Look at the paragraph beginning: *Eventually, the sun began to set...*
What increased Beth's anxiety?

....

Practice Questions — Story

8   The moods of the characters change during the story.

    a)   Look at the paragraph beginning: *They set off, and when they reached...*
        Find and copy the words that show where Richard's mood changes.

        ....

        ....

    b)   How does Richard's mood change at this point?

        ....

        ....

9   Which of the following best describes Richard?

                                                  Tick **one** box.

He is arrogant and stubborn.   ☐

He is a good friend.   ☐

He is aggressive.   ☐

He is kind and honest.   ☐

10   **Find** and **copy two** different words that suggest Beth was angry with Richard after they arrived back at the cafe.

        ....

11   Based on what you have read, what do you think the characters might do next?

        ....

        ....

Practice Questions — Non-Fiction

The Marathon

The marathon is a long-distance running event that is held in countries across the globe. Although the first marathon was held in 1896, the event's origins go back thousands of years to the time of the ancient Greeks. According to legend, an ancient Greek messenger ran approximately 25 miles from the Battle of Marathon to Athens to deliver the news that the Greeks had been victorious. This story inspired the marathon that we know today.

Nowadays, the marathon's distance is set at 26.2 miles. This exact distance was first run at the 1908 Olympic Games, when the race started at Windsor Castle and finished directly in front of the royal box at the Olympic stadium. This extended the course from 25 miles to 26.2 miles, which became the official marathon distance in 1921.

It is not only professional athletes at the Olympic Games who can compete in marathons; these races are often held on public roads in cities, where amateur athletes can also compete. Common reasons for running a marathon include raising money for charity or simply for a sense of achievement.

One of the world's most famous marathons is held annually on the streets of London and was first organised by athletes Chris Brasher and John Disley. They were inspired by the New York City Marathon to create their own marathon event. The first London Marathon was held in 1981, when over 6000 people completed the race. Its popularity has grown massively since then, with tens of thousands of people now running each year. The total number of race finishers in London now stands at over one million.

Many variations of the marathon have been developed over the years. Runners can choose to make the event even more gruelling by running further than the marathon distance in an ultra-marathon, or they could instead opt for a shorter 13.1 mile course: a half-marathon. Athletes can also complete a marathon as part of a triathlon, where they swim, cycle and then run.

Practice Questions — Non-Fiction

There are some less traditional marathons held around the world. The Big Five Marathon in South Africa has a course that winds through the habitat of rhinos, buffalo, lions, elephants and leopards. There is also a marathon held in China where athletes run part of the course on top of the Great Wall of China.

Training for a marathon requires dedication. It can take months for an athlete to build up the fitness needed to run such a long distance. But whether a runner completes an ultra-marathon, a regular marathon, or races alongside lions and leopards, they will no doubt find it a rewarding experience.

1   Look at the first paragraph.
What does the word *legend* tell you about the story of the Greek messenger?

....

....

2   Where did the marathon get its name from?

....

3   How long is a marathon today?

....

Practice Questions — Non-Fiction

4 Where did the marathon at the 1908 Olympic Games start?

....

5 According to the text, what are two common reasons someone might want to complete a marathon? Give **two** reasons.

....

....

6 Look at the paragraph beginning *One of the world's...* **Find** and **copy** one word meaning once a year.

....

7 How many people completed the first London Marathon?

....

Practice Questions — Non-Fiction

8   What is an *ultra-marathon*?

Tick **one** box.

A run that is half the distance of a marathon.   ☐

A run that is longer than a marathon.   ☐

A run that is combined with a swim and a cycle.   ☐

A marathon that is completed in London.   ☐

9   What makes the Big Five Marathon *less traditional*?

....

10   Why does training for a marathon require *dedication*?

....

11   Read each sentence and tick one box to show whether it is a **fact** or an **opinion**.

Sentence	Fact	Opinion
Chris Brasher and John Disley set up the London Marathon.		
The London Marathon is famous.		
The most spectacular marathon on the planet takes place in China.		
People will find running a marathon rewarding.		

Practice Questions — Poem

Read this poem, then answer the questions below.

Something Told the Wild Geese

Something told the wild geese
It was time to go;
Though the fields lay golden
Something whispered, — 'snow'.

Leaves were green and stirring,
Berries, luster-glossed,
But beneath warm feathers
Something cautioned, — 'frost'.

All the sagging orchards
Steamed with amber spice,
But each wild breast stiffened
At remembered ice.

Something told the wild geese
It was time to fly —
Summer sun was on their wings,
Winter in their cry.

Rachel Lyman Field

1   **Find** and **copy** a word that shows that the leaves were moving.

....

2   Why are the geese leaving when the weather is still warm?

Tick **one** box.

They were too warm.   ☐

They were forced to leave.   ☐

They could tell that cold weather was coming.   ☐

There was nothing for them to eat.   ☐

Practice Questions — Poem

3   **Find** and **copy** a word which shows that there is a lot of fruit in the orchards.

....

4   How can you tell that the geese have experienced cold weather before?

....

5   **Find** and **copy** two words which suggest that cold weather can be dangerous for geese.

....

6   Look at the final verse. **Find** and **copy** a phrase that shows the poem takes place in summer.

....

7   What is the overall message of the text?

Tick **one** box.

Geese like to travel.   ☐

Geese know to leave before winter arrives.   ☐

Geese are afraid of winter.   ☐

Geese prefer warm climates.   ☐

Nouns

Common Nouns are Things

Common nouns are everyday words for things. They can be singular or plural.

> zebra   chef   calendar
>
> flowers   balloon   buses

Proper Nouns are Names

Proper nouns are names for particular people, places or things, like days or months.
Proper nouns always need a capital letter.

> On Tuesday, Hannah is going to London to see Big Ben.

These are all examples of proper nouns.

Some Nouns are Harder to Spot

1)   Some nouns are special names for groups of things.
     They are words like 'team', 'herd', 'pack' and 'crowd'.

> The flock of sheep followed the snowman.

2)   Some nouns are names of things that you can't see,
     touch, taste, smell or hear, like ideas and emotions.

> Joy and laughter filled the air when he told us the good news.

EXAMPLE: ∙∙∙∙∙∙∙∙∙∙∙∙∙∙∙∙∙∙∙∙∙∙∙∙∙∙∙∙∙∙∙∙∙∙∙∙∙∙

Read the sentence below. Underline all of the nouns.

> The best teachers show humour and kindness.

'Humour' and 'kindness' are still nouns, even if you can't see them.

"I can identify different types of noun."

Verbs

Verbs are Doing or Being Words

Verbs are <u>action</u> words — they show what a person or thing is <u>doing</u> or <u>being</u>.

> We <u>run</u> around in circles.

> Sarah and James <u>are</u> electricians.

Whoever's <u>doing the verb</u> in a sentence is the <u>subject</u>. The <u>object</u> has the verb done <u>to it</u>.

> <u>The cat</u> sits on <u>the sofa</u>.

the <u>subject</u>   the <u>object</u>

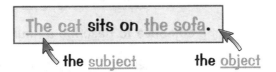

<u>Passive</u> sentences are a bit different. Have a look on p.**33**.

The Subject and the Verb Have to Agree

<u>Verbs change</u> depending on <u>who's</u> doing the action.

> <u>They sail</u> across the lake.   <u>Herbert goes</u> down the stairs.

Most verbs <u>stay the same</u> if '<u>I</u>', '<u>you</u>', '<u>we</u>' or '<u>they</u>' are doing the action, but they <u>change</u> for '<u>he</u>', '<u>she</u>' and '<u>it</u>'.

Modal Verbs Can Show Possibility

Modal verbs like '<u>may</u>', '<u>might</u>' and '<u>shall</u>' can show how <u>likely</u> things are.

> She <u>shall</u> <u>fix</u> your guitar.

'<u>Shall</u>' is the <u>modal verb</u>.   '<u>Fix</u>' is the <u>main verb</u> in the sentence.

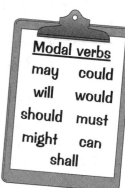

Modal verbs	
may	could
will	would
should	must
might	can
shall	

EXAMPLE: Read the sentence below. Underline the two <u>modal verbs</u>.

> I <u>will</u> play badminton on Tuesday, but I <u>might</u> clean my room first.

"I know what verbs are and how to use them."

Adjectives

Adjectives Describe Nouns

You need to be able to spot an <u>adjective</u> in a sentence. Just remember, it always <u>describes</u> the <u>noun</u>.

> The <u>stale</u> bread tasted funny.

> Gregory is a <u>terrible</u> golfer.

You can use <u>more than one</u> adjective to <u>describe</u> a noun.

> The barn was <u>old</u> and <u>crumbling</u>.

Adjectives can be separated by '<u>and</u>'...

> The ghost floated into the <u>old</u>, <u>crumbling</u> barn.

... or they can be separated by <u>commas</u>.

Adjectives Can Go Before or After the Noun

Adjectives can be found in <u>different parts</u> of a sentence.

> The <u>blue</u> bike was <u>rusty</u> and its brakes were <u>squeaky</u>.

This comes <u>before</u> the noun it describes.   These come <u>after</u> the nouns they describe.

EXAMPLE:

Read the sentences below. Underline all of the <u>adjectives</u>.

Wesley is a <u>brilliant</u> guitarist. His music is <u>great</u> and his band will be <u>famous</u> one day.

Sometimes They Come From Other Words

Sometimes adjectives are made from <u>nouns</u> or <u>verbs</u>. You often need to add an <u>ending</u> like '<u>ful</u>' or '<u>less</u>' to make an adjective.

| <u>pain</u> | + | <u>ful</u> | = | <u>painful</u> |
| noun | | ending | | adjective |

"I know what adjectives are and how to use them."

Adverbs

Adverbs Describe Verbs

Adverbs tell you <u>how</u>, <u>where</u>, <u>when</u> or <u>why</u> an action was done. They often end in '<u>ly</u>'.

Stacey hummed <u>quietly</u> as she was working.

Adverbs can go <u>before</u> or <u>after</u> the verb. They can also go at the <u>start</u> of a <u>sentence</u>.

<u>Unfortunately</u>, the moose escaped.

EXAMPLE: Underline the <u>adverb</u> in this sentence.

Geoffrey <u>angrily</u> kicked his book.

The word '<u>angrily</u>' is the adverb. It tells you <u>how</u> Geoffrey kicked the book.

Sometimes, <u>a group of words</u> tells you more about an action. This is called an <u>adverbial</u>.

Alicia tapped her foot <u>in time to the music</u>.

'In time to the music' is an <u>adverbial</u>.

Look Out For Adverbs That Show You When

1) Adverbs like '<u>tomorrow</u>', '<u>late</u>' and '<u>now</u>' show <u>when</u> something happens.

Mifta will go <u>next</u>. Kyle walked home <u>yesterday</u>.

2) Adverbs like '<u>always</u>', '<u>never</u>', '<u>rarely</u>', '<u>sometimes</u>' or '<u>often</u>' tell you how <u>regularly</u> something happens.

I <u>rarely</u> eat chocolate. Fiona <u>often</u> rides to work.

Adverbs Can Show How Likely Something is

Words like '<u>maybe</u>', '<u>perhaps</u>' and '<u>probably</u>' show how <u>likely</u> something is.

I'll <u>definitely</u> play tennis tomorrow.

The adverb '<u>definitely</u>' suggests something is <u>more likely</u> to happen than '<u>maybe</u>'.

<u>Maybe</u> I'll play tennis tomorrow.

"I know what adverbs are and how to use them."

Prepositions

Prepositions Can Tell You Where

1) Prepositions show <u>how</u> things in a sentence are <u>related</u> to each other.

2) Some prepositions tell you <u>where</u> things are in relation to <u>other things</u>.

in   over   into
through   on   at   under

My phone fell <u>into</u> my drink.

The bird hid <u>behind</u> the captain.

These prepositions tell you <u>where</u> someone or something is.

EXAMPLE: Read the sentences below. Underline the <u>prepositions</u>.

The goat stood <u>in</u> the field.

They drove <u>through</u> the tunnel.

She was <u>under</u> the umbrella.

Words like '<u>in</u>', '<u>through</u>' and '<u>under</u>' tell you <u>where</u> the action is taking place.

Prepositions Can Be About Time

Other prepositions tell you <u>when</u> things happen in relation to <u>each other</u>.

She painted the picture <u>on</u> Friday.

<u>During</u> the summer, we go sailing.

until   before   in   during

since   on   after

EXAMPLE:

Complete the sentence below by filling in the gap with a <u>preposition</u>.

He puts on his shirt ....<u>before</u>.... his trousers.

You could also put '<u>after</u>' here.

"I know what prepositions are and how to use them."

Pronouns

Pronouns Replace Nouns

1) Pronouns save you from repeating a noun over and over again.

2) Pronouns like 'they', 'we' and 'me' can replace nouns in a sentence.

> Mark gave his sister the bike, but she didn't like it.

The pronoun 'she' replaces 'his sister'.

The pronoun 'it' replaces 'the bike'.

3) Be careful — sometimes it's not clear who you're talking about:

> Raj told Guy that he couldn't go to the party.

It's not clear if it's Raj or Guy who won't be at the party.

There Are Two Main Groups of Pronouns

Use these if the person or thing is doing the action.

| I | you | he | she | it | we | they |

The pronouns for 'you' and 'it' are the same.

| me | you | him | her | it | us | them |

Use these if the person or thing is having the action done to it.

EXAMPLE: Write down a pronoun to replace the underlined word.

> The ball flew towards Roger and hit Roger on the back of the head.

'Roger' is having the action done to him, so the pronoun has to be 'him'.

him

Some Pronouns Show Belonging

Possessive pronouns show who owns something.

> My car broke down, so Bob lent me his.

'His' replaces 'his car'.

mine hers
yours ours
his theirs

"I know what pronouns are and how to use them."

Determiners

Determiners Go Before Nouns

1) Determiners are small words that go before nouns.

2) An article is one type of determiner. There are three articles: 'a', 'an' and 'the'. Use 'a' and 'an' for general things and 'the' for specific things.

> Angus ate a fish.

This could be any fish.

> Angus ate the fish.

This means a specific fish.

3) Use 'a' when the next word starts with a consonant sound, and 'an' when the next word starts with a vowel sound.

> a mouse   an igloo   a unicorn

'Unicorn' sounds like it could start with a 'y'. This is a consonant sound, so it goes with 'a'.

EXAMPLE: Fill in the gap with the appropriate determiner.

> The aliens could see ...the..... Moon from their spaceship.

The correct answer is 'the' because it refers to something specific.

Here Are Some Other Types of Determiner

There are other types of determiner, which all have different jobs to do.

1) They can show whether a noun is specific or general:

This means a specific pair of shoes. → He gave me these shoes.

Do you want some pizza? ← This could be any pizza.

2) They can show how many things there are, or if someone owns something:

> There are six lemurs.

> Solomon forgot his lunch.

"I know what determiners are and how to use them."

Practice Questions

1 Write your own sentence using the word '**offer**' as a **noun**.
Don't change the word, and use the correct punctuation in your sentence.

....

Write your own sentence using the word '**offer**' as a **verb**.
Don't change the word, and use the correct punctuation in your sentence.

....

2 Underline the two **modal verbs** in the sentence below.

Omar should study for the test, but he might go to the cinema instead.

3 Complete the sentence below by filling in the gap with an appropriate **adjective**.

Patrick and Carmen were clever, but they were ....

4 Read the passage below. Write an **adjective** derived from the noun in brackets in each space. One has already been done for you.

Sebastian went on holiday with his family to a ....*beautiful*.... [**beauty**] part of the

countryside. They rented a house in an area that was .... [**hill**], but

close to the local village. They had a very .... [**peace**] holiday.

5 Put a tick in each row of the table below to show whether the words in bold are **adjectives** or **adverbs**.

Sentence	Adjective	Adverb
Julia **regularly** runs along the canal.		
Tightrope walkers are **fearless** people.		
Perhaps tomorrow we can go to the beach.		

6 Read the sentence below and circle the two **adverbs**.

Shirley must run quickly to the station because the train leaves soon.

Practice Questions

7   Read the sentences below. Choose a **preposition** from the box to fill each gap and write it on the line. You can only use each preposition **once**.

until	under	through

Fatima heard a strange noise and hid .... the bed. She stayed there

.... four o'clock. When she eventually looked .... the

window, she saw a strange, dark shape moving towards her.

8   Read the sentences below. Replace the words that are underlined with the correct **pronouns**.

I liked the old clock, so the woman gave <u>the old clock</u> to me for free.

John loved the theatre, so <u>John</u> went to London to see a musical.

9   Read the sentence below. Tick the pair of **pronouns** that best completes the sentence.

My family and our neighbours each own a bouncy castle. .... keep ours inside, but .... is so big that it has to stay outside.

Tick **one** box.

Ours	they	☐
We	theirs	☐
Theirs	ours	☐
They	we	☐

10   Read the sentence below and circle all the **determiners**.

The cabbages look great, but we need a leek to complete the recipe.

Sentences

Statements Usually Give Information

Statements are sentences which tell you something.
The word types in a statement are usually in the same order.

The woman sweeps the rubbish.

Statements usually
end with a full stop.

The subject usually
comes first (the person
or thing doing the verb).

The verb
comes next.

The object usually comes after
the verb. It's the person or thing
that the verb is being done to.

Questions Always Ask About Something

Questions often start with a question word.

When is your birthday?

Questions
always end in a
question mark.

who   how   what
        when
which   why   where

Sometimes statements can be rearranged to make questions:

He is here. ⟶ Is he here?

Question tags can turn statements into
questions. Find out more on p.36.

Questions like this don't need a question word, but they do need a question mark.

Commands Give Instructions or Orders

Commands tell people what to do. They always have a verb that gives an order.

Stand over there.

Bring me an ice cream!

Commands can end in
an exclamation mark
or a full stop.

These are the verbs that give the order.

Exclamations Show Strong Feelings

Exclamations show strong feelings like surprise, pain or anger.
They always start with either 'what' or 'how' and must have a verb.

How selfish Jay is!

What long hair you have!

Exclamations usually have an exclamation mark.

"I can identify different types of sentence."

Clauses and Phrases

Sentences Are Made of Clauses and Phrases

A <u>clause</u> is part of a sentence which has a <u>subject</u> and a <u>verb</u>.

<u>Ollie swims</u> in the pool.

This is a <u>clause</u> because it has a <u>verb</u> ('<u>swims</u>') and a <u>subject</u> ('<u>Ollie</u>').

A <u>phrase</u> is part of a sentence, usually <u>without a verb</u>.

Ollie swims <u>in the pool</u>.

This is a <u>phrase</u>. It doesn't contain a verb.

Sentences Are Built Around a Main Clause

1) A <u>main clause</u> is a clause that would <u>make sense</u> as a <u>separate sentence</u>.

Rufus went to the dentist. — This is a <u>main clause</u>.

2) <u>Subordinate clauses</u> add <u>extra information</u> to a sentence. They usually start with a <u>conjunction</u> like '<u>while</u>' or '<u>because</u>'.

<u>Rufus went to the dentist</u> <u>because he had toothache</u>.

The <u>main clause</u> is the <u>main idea</u> of the sentence.

The <u>subordinate clause</u> adds extra information to the sentence.

3) Sometimes a <u>subordinate clause</u> comes <u>before</u> the main clause.

<u>Because he had toothache</u>, <u>Rufus went to the dentist</u>.

You need a comma <u>after</u> the <u>subordinate clause</u>.

EXAMPLE: Read the sentence below. Underline the <u>main clause</u>.

<u>The parrot flew for miles</u> until it found somewhere to land.

This is the <u>main clause</u> that you'd underline.
The rest of the sentence is the <u>subordinate clause</u>.

Clauses and Phrases

Subordinate Clauses Don't Work Alone

Main clauses make sense on their own.
Subordinate clauses don't make sense on their own.

Sophia cooked a meal because the restaurant was closed.

main clause   subordinate clause

Sophia cooked a meal.

Because the restaurant was closed.

The main clause makes sense
as a sentence on its own.

The subordinate clause doesn't make sense
on its own — it isn't a full sentence.

Noun Phrases Describe Things

A noun phrase is a type of phrase that includes a noun and any words that describe it.

the messy baby

the messy baby with blonde hair

Both of these
examples are
noun phrases.

You can add adjectives, prepositions or other nouns to expand a noun phrase.

the messy baby beside the bowl of pudding

This is a preposition phrase.
It starts with a preposition and
gives you more information.

Adverbial Phrases Tell You About Actions

An adverbial phrase is a group of words that acts like an adverb in a sentence. They can
describe why, when, where and how often something happens. They're also called adverbials.

She cooks the rice
every day at noon.

After the show, we
went out for dinner.

He went to the
meeting at the library.

"I can identify different clauses and phrases."

Conjunctions

Conjunctions Join Things Together

1) Conjunctions are <u>linking words</u> — they can be used to <u>join</u> clauses or phrases to each other.

2) Two <u>main clauses</u> can be joined together by adding a <u>co-ordinating conjunction</u> like '<u>and</u>', '<u>but</u>' or '<u>or</u>'.

Matthew drank juice <u>and</u> Maria dug a hole.

The <u>conjunction</u> joins the two clauses together into <u>one sentence</u>.

The bird flew away, <u>so</u> I couldn't see it anymore.

Grace loves tomato juice, <u>but</u> she hates tomato soup.

Some co-ordinating conjunctions

yet   or   so
but   and

Others Join Main and Subordinate Clauses

Some sentences are made from a <u>main clause</u> and a <u>subordinate clause</u>. These are normally joined together by <u>subordinating conjunctions</u>.

Some subordinating conjunctions

if   although   while
until   because

I'm going to stay at home <u>because</u> it's raining.

This <u>conjunction</u> shows that a <u>subordinate clause</u> is about to <u>begin</u>.

He won't go <u>unless</u> you go too.

<u>Before</u> her mum came home, Milly painted the living room.

When the subordinate clause comes <u>before</u> the main clause, the <u>conjunction</u> goes at the <u>start</u> of the <u>sentence</u>.

EXAMPLE:

Read the sentence below. Underline the two <u>conjunctions</u>.

<u>Although</u> he was tired, Jim ran outside <u>because</u> he saw an ice cream van.

'<u>Although</u>' and '<u>because</u>' are both <u>subordinating conjunctions</u>.

"I can link ideas together using conjunctions."

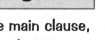

Active and Passive

Active Sentences Focus On Who

Most sentences are in the <u>active voice</u> — it's clear <u>who</u> is doing the action.
The <u>subject</u> does something <u>to</u> the <u>object</u>.

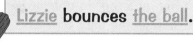
Lizzie bounces the ball.

Lizzie is <u>doing</u> the action.
She's the <u>subject</u>.

<u>The ball</u> is having the action
done <u>to it</u>. It's the <u>object</u>.

Passive Sentences Focus On What

When a sentence is in the <u>passive voice</u>, something is <u>done to</u> the subject.

<u>The ball</u> was thrown <u>by Henry</u>. The word '<u>by</u>' can introduce
<u>who</u> does the action.

the subject

<u>The goal</u> was scored <u>by Angela</u> just before the game ended.

You <u>don't</u> always need to say who does the action in <u>passive</u> sentences.
'The goal was scored just before the game ended' makes sense too.

EXAMPLE: Read the sentences below. Tick a box in each row to show whether
the sentence is written in the <u>active</u> voice or the <u>passive</u> voice.

In this sentence, the <u>subject</u>
(Amy) is <u>doing something</u> (posting)
to the <u>object</u> (the letter).

In the second sentence,
the <u>subject</u> (Mera) is
<u>doing something</u> (watering)
to the <u>objects</u> (the plants).

In the last sentence, the <u>subject</u>
(the lion) is having something
done <u>to it</u> (being fed).

Sentence	Active	Passive
Amy posted the letter.	✓	
Mera watered the plants.	✓	
The lion was fed by the zookeeper.		✓

"I can identify active and passive sentences."

Tenses

Verb Tenses Tell You When

1) The tense of a verb tells you <u>when</u> something happens.

2) The verb <u>changes</u> in the different tenses.

This is the <u>simple present tense.</u> I <u>wait</u>.

You can often add '<u>ed</u>' to change a verb to the <u>simple past tense.</u> I <u>waited</u>.

3) <u>Not all</u> verbs follow the '<u>add ed</u>' rule. Take these, for example:

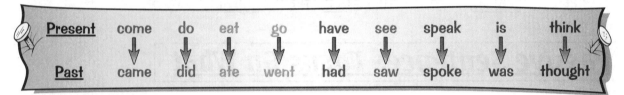

Present	come	do	eat	go	have	see	speak	is	think
Past	came	did	ate	went	had	saw	spoke	was	thought

EXAMPLE:

Fill in the gaps below by changing the verbs in boxes to the <u>simple past tense.</u>

I __went__ to the cinema last week and I __watched__ 'Tiger Prawns 3'.

go — Remember that 'go' <u>doesn't</u> follow the 'add ed' rule.

watch

Use 'To Be' With 'ing' Verbs

1) To show an action is <u>currently happening</u>, you use the <u>present progressive</u> form. This is made using part of the verb '<u>to be</u>' and an '<u>ing</u>' verb.

The part of '<u>to be</u>' ('<u>is</u>') is in the <u>present tense</u>. This means that the 'ing' verb is <u>happening right now</u>.

He <u>is</u> <u>riding</u> his horse.

The present progressive is a type of present tense.

The '<u>ing</u>' part tells you <u>what</u> the action is.

2) You can also use the <u>simple past tense</u> of '<u>to be</u>' to make the <u>past progressive</u> form.

The past progressive is a type of past tense.

He <u>was</u> <u>riding</u> his horse.

'<u>Was</u>' is in the <u>past tense</u>. This means the action was happening <u>in the past</u>.

Tenses

You Can Use 'Have' to Make the Perfect Form

To talk about things that have <u>already happened</u>, use the <u>simple present tense</u> of '<u>have</u>'.

She <u>has</u> <u>bought</u> three balloons.

This is the <u>present perfect</u> form. It is a type of <u>present tense</u>.

'<u>Has</u>' is in the <u>present tense</u>.

The girl has <u>already</u> bought the balloons. The verb is in the <u>past tense</u>.

EXAMPLE: Tick the sentence that uses the <u>present perfect form</u>.

The cafe is open from nine o'clock until early evening. ☐

He was on his way home when he dropped his keys. ☐

She drove along the coast because she wanted to see the sea. ☐

The police <u>have</u> managed to evacuate the area. ☑

The present tense of '<u>have</u>' shows that this is the <u>perfect form</u>.

Be Consistent with Tenses

1) Verb tenses need to be <u>consistent</u>. If there is <u>no change in time</u>, verbs should <u>stay</u> in the same tense <u>throughout the sentence</u>.

Daisy <u>rushed</u> to the front door and <u>picked</u> up the parcel.

2) However, if the <u>time changes</u>, then the <u>verb tense</u> may also <u>change</u>.

EXAMPLE: Which two verbs correctly complete the sentence below?

Sid ..... pink hair <u>yesterday</u>, but <u>today</u> he ..... orange hair.

The time changes here, so the tense needs to change.

has   has   had   had   has   had   <u>had</u>   <u>has</u>

This is the correct answer — <u>past</u> (had) then <u>present</u> (has).

"I can recognise and use different tenses."

Formal and Informal Writing

Formal and Informal Texts are Different

Formal writing uses more complicated words than informal writing:

> Ray is a rubbish superhero.

> Ray is a disastrous superhero.

'Disastrous' is more complicated than 'rubbish'.

Contracted Forms aren't Formal

Contracted forms, like 'isn't' and 'I'm', are only used in informal texts. In formal writing, write them out in full.

For more about contracted forms, see p.42.

> I didn't finish the test in time.

informal

> I did not finish the test in time.

formal

Question Tags Are Used in Informal Texts

Informal writing sometimes uses question tags.

> That smells awful, doesn't it?

The question tag 'doesn't it' turns this sentence into a question.

EXAMPLE: Read the sentences below. Tick the two sentences which are formal.

I can't find my French dictionary. ☐

Jade asked for chips, didn't she? ☐

The contraction 'can't' and question tag 'didn't she' mean the first two sentences are informal.

May we see the menu please? ✓

Miguel responded to the question. ✓

'May' and 'responded' are formal language, so the last two sentences are formal.

"I can recognise formal and informal writing."

Standard and Non-Standard English

Make Sure Your Verbs Are Correct

1) Standard English is correct English. It's the type of writing you should use in your written work. Non-Standard English is a more informal type of English.

2) In Standard English, the verb has to agree with whoever's doing the action.

| You goes to school tomorrow. | → should be → | You go to school tomorrow. |

3) Don't mix up the simple past tense and the present perfect either. You usually need 'have' or 'has' with verbs like 'seen' or 'done'.

| I seen her. | → should be → | I have seen her. | **OR** | I saw her. |

Don't Forget the 'ly' at the End of Adverbs

Dropping the 'ly' from the end of an adverb is non-Standard English.

| Manfred runs funny. | → should be → | Manfred runs funnily. |

EXAMPLE:

Read the sentences below. Underline the correct word in brackets to complete each sentence using Standard English.

You will have to run (quick/quickly) to catch me!

← This is an adverb, so it needs an ly ending.

I (been/was) down by the river. ← Don't mix up tenses in Standard English.

Double Negatives Can Be Confusing

Writing two negatives in the same sentence is called a double negative. Using them can make your sentences confusing.

| I've not got nothing to say. | ← 'Not' and 'nothing' are both negative words. This sentence is very confusing.

Instead, this sentence can be written in Standard English as:

| I've got nothing to say. | | I haven't got anything to say. |

"I know the difference between Standard and non-Standard English."

Practice Questions

1   Draw lines to match each sentence with the correct **function**.
    Each function box should only be used **once**.

Ewen has an expensive camera	command
What a scary robot that is	statement
Put your rubbish in the bin	exclamation
Do you have a pet guinea pig	question

2   Underline the **subject** in each of these sentences.

Later that day, Marie decided to play football.

Despite the hot weather, he was wearing a woolly jumper.

Pancakes are delicious with some maple syrup.

3   Read the sentence below.
    What is '**while we watched from the window**' an example of?

The trees shook violently in the wind **while we watched from the window**.

Tick **one** box.

an adverbial phrase   ☐

a noun phrase   ☐

a subordinate clause   ☐

a main clause   ☐

4   Read the sentences below. Underline all the **conjunctions**.

While Eliza was away, Mario sneaked into her room to play

with her toys. He put everything back, but Eliza still knew.

Practice Questions

5 Read the sentences below. Tick the sentence which is written in the **active voice**.

Tick **one** box.

The parcel was delivered on Friday night. ☐

Trevor and Danielle were given money by their gran. ☐

The choir sang the songs beautifully. ☐

The play was performed by the local theatre group. ☐

6 Read the sentences below. Tick the sentence which is in the **past tense**.

Tick **one** box.

My sister is knitting me a cardigan. ☐

The teacher told the children to stop talking. ☐

My dad is originally from Sweden. ☐

I know all about the history of my town. ☐

7 Read the sentence below.
Circle the two words that show the **tense** in the sentence.

After school, I did my homework then played my violin.

8 Read the sentence below. Replace the underlined word with a **more formal** word. Write the word in the box.

Edith's stepfather was <u>fuming</u> because nobody had washed the dishes.

☐

9 Read the sentences below.
Circle the correct word in brackets to complete each sentence.

Oliver looked at his notes during the test and the teacher **(saw / seen)** him.

Cherie ties her shoes **(weirdly / weird)**.

Hassan had not seen **(nobody / anybody)** in the park all evening.

Punctuating Sentences

New Sentences Start with a Capital Letter

1) <u>Every sentence</u> has to <u>start</u> with a <u>capital letter</u>.

<u>T</u>he weather has been quite wet. <u>I</u>t has rained every day this week. <u>A</u>ll of the streets are covered in puddles.

2) Some words always start with a <u>capital letter</u>.

<u>M</u>ary went to meet <u>M</u>r <u>D</u>avies in <u>W</u>ales. She arrived on <u>T</u>hursday and got caught in the <u>A</u>pril showers. Later that week, <u>I</u> went to join them.

<u>I</u> is always written with a capital letter, no matter where it is in a sentence.

<u>Proper nouns</u> always start with a capital letter too (see p.20).

Other Punctuation Marks Finish Sentences

1) To show where a sentence ends, use a <u>full stop</u>: .

2) If the sentence shows <u>strong feelings</u>, like <u>surprise</u> or <u>anger</u>, replace the full stop with an <u>exclamation mark</u>: !

3) If the sentence is a <u>question</u>, use a <u>question mark</u>: ?

> **EXAMPLE:** Choose a <u>punctuation mark</u> to finish each of these sentences.

A cow was walking along the road.

There is a cow on the road!

This sentence is showing a strong emotion, so it ends with an <u>exclamation mark</u>.

Why is there a cow on the road?

This is a <u>question</u>, so it ends with a <u>question mark</u>.

"I can use capital letters, full stops, exclamation marks and question marks."

Commas

Commas go Between Items in a List

This is a <u>comma</u>:

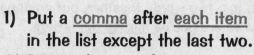

You use commas to <u>separate</u> <u>things</u> in a <u>list</u>. Just follow these handy rules:

1) Put a <u>comma</u> after <u>each item</u> in the list except the last two.
2) Put '<u>and</u>' or '<u>or</u>' between the last two items.

EXAMPLE: Add <u>commas</u> to the sentence below so that it is punctuated correctly.

Sam and Adeela took sandwiches, apples, bananas <u>and</u> cakes on their picnic.

Commas go after <u>each item</u> in the <u>list</u>.

'And' goes between the <u>last two items</u> instead.

Commas help you Add Extra Information

Commas are also used to join an <u>adverbial</u> to the front of a sentence:

After lunch, Sharlene played cricket.

Adverbial — Comma

See page 31 for more on adverbials.

They can also make Sentences Clear

Commas can <u>break up</u> sentences to make the <u>meaning clear</u>.

After meeting Umair, Stacy and the policeman had lunch.

This suggests that a <u>policeman</u> and a girl called Stacy met Umair, then had lunch.

Adding a <u>comma</u> after 'meeting' changes the <u>meaning</u> of the sentence.

After meeting, Umair, Stacy and the policeman had lunch.

Now, it suggests that Umair, Stacy and the policeman met <u>all together</u>.

"I can use commas to separate items in lists, after adverbials and to make sentences clearer."

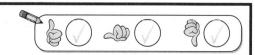

Apostrophes

Apostrophes _join_ Two Words _Together_

This is an <u>apostrophe</u>: ,

When you <u>join two words</u> together, put an <u>apostrophe</u> in to show where you've <u>missed out letters</u>.

1) When two words are <u>joined together</u> with an apostrophe, a <u>new word</u> is created.

2) This is called the <u>contracted form</u>.

<u>Contracted forms</u> are only for <u>informal writing</u>. They can also be called <u>contractions</u>.

EXAMPLE: Write the <u>contracted forms</u> of the words on the left of each column, using <u>apostrophes</u> in the correct places.

I will	I'll	..........I did not	I didn't
I have	I've	..........I will not	I won't
Let us	Let's	..........I cannot	I can't

'<u>I won't</u>' doesn't quite match the missing letters of '<u>I will not</u>'.

Apostrophes _show Something Belongs_

To show who owns something (<u>possession</u>), you add an <u>apostrophe</u> and an '<u>s</u>' to the <u>owner's name</u>.

1) If there is only <u>one owner</u>, add an <u>apostrophe</u> and an '<u>s</u>'.

Sarah<u>'s</u> car broke down.   The monster<u>'s</u> head fell off.

2) If something <u>belongs</u> to a <u>group of people</u>, then follow these two rules.

If the plural word <u>ends</u> in '<u>s</u>', <u>just</u> add an <u>apostrophe</u>.   The bankers<u>'</u> lunches were stolen.

If the plural word <u>doesn't</u> end in '<u>s</u>', add an <u>apostrophe</u> and an '<u>s</u>'.   The women<u>'s</u> race was cancelled.

"I can use apostrophes to make contracted forms and to show possession."

Inverted Commas

Inverted Commas show Someone is Speaking

These are <u>inverted commas</u>: " "

1) <u>Inverted commas</u> can also be called <u>speech marks</u>.

2) You put them around <u>direct speech</u>.

Direct speech is when you write down the exact words that someone says.

"<u>H</u>e passed all of his exams!" said Jacqui.

Use a <u>capital letter</u> when someone <u>starts</u> to speak.

Speech always Ends with a Punctuation Mark

1) <u>Speech ends</u> with a <u>comma</u>, <u>full stop</u>, <u>exclamation mark</u> or <u>question mark</u>.

2) Put this punctuation <u>inside</u> the speech marks.

Inverted commas go at the <u>start</u> and <u>end</u> of speech.

"I need to get away," said Pirate Sid.

If the sentence <u>carries on</u> after the speech, put a <u>comma</u> (unless it's a question or exclamation).

If the sentence <u>ends</u> with the speech, you need a <u>comma before</u> the <u>speech starts</u>.

The captain said, "He has stolen all of my gold!"

Start speech with a <u>capital letter</u> when someone new begins to speak.

If the sentence <u>ends</u> when the speech ends, use a <u>full stop</u>, an <u>exclamation mark</u> or a <u>question mark</u>.

EXAMPLE: Add a pair of <u>inverted commas</u> to the sentence below so that it is punctuated correctly.

"Come back with my gold, Pirate Sid!" yelled the captain.

The inverted commas go <u>around</u> what is being said.

"I can punctuate speech correctly."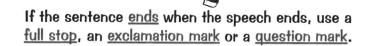

Colons, Semi-Colons and Dashes

Colons Introduce Explanations

This is a <u>colon</u>: ⟶ **:**

Some <u>colons</u> show that you're about to <u>explain a point</u> you've <u>just made</u>.
They normally <u>join together</u> two main clauses.

First Point: More Specific Point

This bit should
<u>make sense</u> on its own.

This is always about the <u>same thing</u> as the <u>first point</u>.
It gives <u>more information</u> or an <u>explanation</u>.

Donald was worried: <u>the water in his footbath was actually cement</u>.

This is the
<u>first point</u>.

The <u>colon</u> goes <u>before</u>
the explanation.

This is the information which
<u>explains</u> the <u>first point</u>.

Colons Can Also Introduce Lists

1) If you're <u>writing a list</u>, a <u>colon</u> shows that the <u>list</u> is about to <u>begin</u>.

For the perfect party, you will need five things:
music, balloons, decorations, presents and lots of food.

This <u>introduces</u>
the <u>list of items</u>.

2) <u>Only</u> use a colon to introduce a list if it follows a <u>main clause</u>.

I want balloons, presents, music,
decorations and lots of food.

This sentence <u>doesn't</u> need
a colon because 'I want' on
its own <u>isn't</u> a main clause.

EXAMPLE: Insert the missing <u>colon</u> so that the sentence is punctuated correctly.

<u>They needed some new equipment for their camping
trip</u>: rucksacks, water bottles, a kettle and a tent.

The <u>colon</u> goes <u>after</u> the <u>main clause</u>.

Colons, Semi-Colons and Dashes

Semi-Colons Break Up Lists

This is a semi-colon: ⟶ **;**

1) Semi-colons break up lists of long phrases or clauses. Unlike commas, you still need to put a semi-colon before the 'and' or 'or' that joins the last two things.

> At the party, I met a granny doing tricks on a motorbike; a man with flowing cape and a golden sword; and a businessman in a suit pretending to be a pilot.

2) Semi-colons also break up lists with other punctuation marks in them.

Some of these clauses already have commas or brackets in them.

> Sandra's favourite hobbies are taking part in motorbike races against her sisters (which she often wins); playing chess with her grandson, Selasi; and taking care of her lovely, big garden.

A semi-colon goes before the 'and' that joins the last two things in the list.

Semi-Colons and Dashes can Join Sentences

1) Semi-colons are used to turn two related sentences into one. Both sentences must be about the same thing and equally important. They must also make sense on their own.

> When the second sentence explains the first sentence, a colon is used instead of a semi-colon (see p.44).

EXAMPLE: Add a semi-colon to the sentence below so that it is punctuated correctly.

> Jessica drank a mug of coffee; Alyssa had tea.

Both clauses are equally important and they're both about the same thing. They could be written as two separate sentences.

2) You can also use a single dash to join together two related main clauses.

> Tom went into the shop — there was a crying man inside.

"I can use colons, semi-colons and dashes correctly."

Adding Extra Information

Brackets give Extra Information...

These are <u>brackets</u>:   **( )**

<u>Brackets</u> go around <u>extra information</u> and keep it <u>separate</u> from the rest of the sentence. They're <u>always</u> used in <u>pairs</u>.

> Mabel and Doris (<u>who are twins</u>) work on the building site.

EXAMPLE: Add a <u>pair of brackets</u> to the sentence below so that it is punctuated correctly.

> Mabel and Doris are the building site's best workers (<u>they work harder than everyone else</u>).

If the <u>closing bracket</u> is at the <u>end</u> of a <u>sentence</u>, it goes <u>before</u> the <u>full stop</u>.

This is the <u>extra information</u> — you could <u>take it out</u> and the sentence would <u>still make sense</u>.

... And Commas and Dashes can too

1) A <u>pair of commas</u> can be used <u>instead of brackets</u> to add <u>extra information</u>.

> The flies, <u>which are always buzzing</u>, were particularly annoying today.

The commas go <u>either side</u> of the extra information.

2) A <u>pair of dashes</u> can be used in the same way.

> Megan — <u>my sister</u> — received her certificate today.

The <u>extra information</u> goes <u>between</u> the dashes.

You can also use a single dash to join two main clauses — see page 45 for more on this.

"I can use brackets, dashes and commas to add extra information."

Hyphens and Bullet Points

Use Hyphens to Avoid Confusion

This is a <u>hyphen</u>: ⟶ **-**

<u>Hyphens</u> can be used to show which word is being <u>described</u> by an adjective. They help to <u>avoid confusion</u>.

I was behind a slow-moving van.

The hyphen shows that the word '<u>slow</u>' <u>describes</u> the word '<u>moving</u>'. This means that the van wasn't moving very quickly.

I was behind a slow moving van.

Removing the hyphen <u>changes</u> the <u>meaning</u> of the sentence. Here, the word '<u>slow</u>' is used to describe a <u>moving van</u>.

EXAMPLE: Which of these sentences uses a hyphen correctly?

Kate saw a friendly-looking cat.

This is <u>correct</u> — the word '<u>friendly</u>' <u>describes</u> the way the cat <u>looks</u>.

Kate saw a friendly looking-cat.

This is <u>incorrect</u> — there's no such thing as a 'looking-cat'.

Bullet Points Break Up Information

<u>Bullet points</u> are used in <u>lists</u> to <u>separate</u> different <u>points</u>.

The hospital has three departments:
• <u>T</u>he Accident and Emergency department
• <u>A</u> General Surgery department
• <u>T</u>he Ear, Nose and Throat (ENT) department

Use a <u>colon</u> to introduce the <u>list</u> of points.

You can also put <u>commas</u> or <u>semi-colons</u> at the end of each bullet point, with a <u>full stop</u> after the final point.

If you use a <u>capital letter</u> at the start of <u>one point</u>, then use capitals at the start of <u>all</u> of the points.

"I can use hyphens and bullet points correctly."

Practice Questions

1   Circle the words which need **capital letters**.

mary seacole was a nurse from jamaica. she was born
in 1805 and died in england on the 14th of may 1881.

2   The sentence below is missing a **punctuation mark** in the place
the arrow is pointing at. Which punctuation mark should be used?

"When does the train arrive " Janice asked.

Tick **one** box.

full stop   ☐

question mark   ☐

comma   ☐

exclamation mark   ☐

3   Insert the missing **comma** so that the sentence is punctuated correctly.

The athlete was fast strong and very determined.

4   Tick the sentence which uses **commas** correctly.

Tick **one** box.

As soon as he could, Mr Andrews called the fire brigade.   ☐

In March the new road, village hall, and
children's playground will be opened.   ☐

After breakfast Lord Aft went to play, cricket with the local club.   ☐

After retiring, as head teacher last year,
Mrs McKinnon started doing part-time work.   ☐

5   Circle the word that includes an **apostrophe** for **possession**.

We'll meet at the gardener's hut on the east side of the park. I've heard
that it is always nice and quiet there, and we've got loads of time to walk.

Practice Questions

6 Tick the sentence that is punctuated correctly.

Tick **one** box.

"It's been raining all day here", said Gabby. ☐

"It's been raining all day here," said Gabby. ☐

It's been raining all day here," said Gabby. ☐

"It's been raining all day here." said Gabby. ☐

7 Look at the table below. Put a tick in each row to show whether each sentence uses a **colon** correctly or incorrectly.

Sentence	Correctly	Incorrectly
I only have a short shopping list: today a loaf of bread, a bunch of bananas and a pint of milk.		
He could count his good friends on one hand: Rory, Rose, Susan, Sarah and Jane.		
I saw a lot of birds yesterday: a thrush, a heron, two starlings, a buzzard and five ducklings.		
The table was filled with food: the chef didn't want any of her customers to go hungry.		

8 Insert a **semi-colon** so that the sentence is punctuated correctly.

Lots of television crews went to the shore they were all hoping to film the monster that lived in the water.

9 Insert a pair of **brackets** so that the sentence is punctuated correctly.

The mechanic who came from the neighbouring village started working on Jeffrey's car.

10 Read the sentence below. Add a **hyphen** between two of the words to show that the rabbit eats mice.

There's a mouse eating rabbit in the garden.

Prefixes

Prefixes Go at the Beginning of a Word

A <u>prefix</u> is a <u>letter</u> or <u>group</u> of letters that goes at the <u>beginning of a word</u> to form a <u>new word</u>.

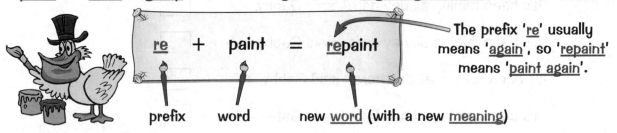

re   +   paint   =   repaint

prefix   word   new <u>word</u> (with a new <u>meaning</u>)

The prefix '<u>re</u>' usually means '<u>again</u>', so '<u>repaint</u>' means '<u>paint again</u>'.

Prefixes Can Give a Word a Different Meaning

1)   <u>Prefixes</u> usually <u>change the meaning</u> of a word.

Karis <u>played</u> the video.   Karis <u>replayed</u> the video.

In this <u>second example</u>, Karis played the video <u>again</u>.

2)   Some prefixes, e.g. '<u>un</u>', give a <u>word</u> the <u>opposite meaning</u>.

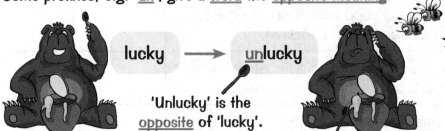

lucky → <u>un</u>lucky

'Unlucky' is the <u>opposite</u> of 'lucky'.

When you add a prefix, the <u>spelling</u> of the original word <u>doesn't change</u>.

3)   Adding a <u>prefix</u> like '<u>super</u>', '<u>anti</u>' or '<u>auto</u>' gives <u>nouns</u> a <u>new meaning</u>.

<u>super</u>market   <u>anti</u>clockwise   <u>auto</u>biography

'<u>Super</u>' usually means '<u>bigger</u>', so a '<u>supermarket</u>' is a '<u>bigger market</u>'.   '<u>Anti</u>' means '<u>opposite</u>', so '<u>anticlockwise</u>' means '<u>the opposite way to clockwise</u>'.   '<u>Auto</u>' means <u>self</u>, so an '<u>autobiography</u>' is something you write about <u>yourself</u>.

4)   Adding '<u>de</u>', '<u>dis</u>' or '<u>re</u>' changes the meaning of <u>verbs</u>.

<u>mis</u>understood

'<u>Mis</u>' often means '<u>wrong</u>' so '<u>misunderstood</u>' means '<u>understood incorrectly</u>'.

<u>dis</u>appear

'<u>Dis</u>' can mean '<u>not</u>', so '<u>disappear</u>' means '<u>not appear</u>'.

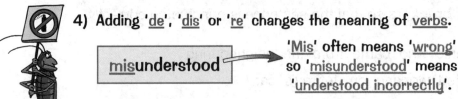

"I know what prefixes are and how they change the meaning of a word."

Suffixes

Suffixes Go at the End of a Word

1) A suffix is a letter or a group of letters that goes at the end of a word.

climb + er = climber

word   suffix   new word (with a new meaning)

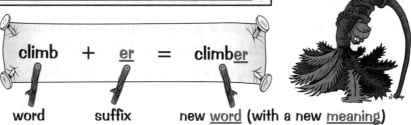

2) Add 's' or 'es' to make a singular noun plural.

Both cats ran away.   There were three buses.

3) Sometimes the spelling changes when a suffix is added to the word.

Kristoff thought his teeth looked beautiful.

The 'y' of 'beauty' has been changed to an 'i'.

Suffixes Form Nouns

A suffix can turn a verb or an adjective into a noun.

| movement | prettiness | skier | complexity |

'Move' is a verb.   'Pretty' is an adjective.   'Ski' is a verb.   'Complex' is an adjective.

EXAMPLE:

Put a different suffix at the end of each word below to make it a noun.

build ....er....   shy ...ness...   appoint ..ment...   'Builder', 'shyness' and 'appointment' are all nouns.

Suffixes Form Verbs and Adverbs

1) You can add suffixes to nouns or adjectives to form verbs.

apologise → 'Apology' is a noun.   purify → 'Pure' is an adjective.   activate → 'Active' is an adjective.

2) Put 'ly' on the end of an adjective to turn it into an adverb.

Secretly, I wanted Rav to win.   The snails raced slowly.

3) Suffixes can also turn verbs and nouns into adjectives (see p.22 for more on this).

"I know what suffixes are and how they change the meaning of a word."

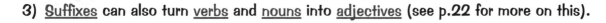

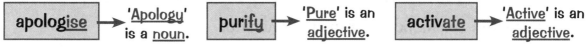

Word Families

Similar Words Make Word Families

1) Words that are from the same <u>word family</u> look like each other — you can usually <u>spot</u> bits of each word that are the <u>same</u>.

2) The part of the word they have in common is called the <u>root</u>.

<u>imag</u>e   <u>imag</u>inary   <u>imag</u>ination

These words all have '<u>imag</u>' as their root.

It might be a bit <u>less obvious</u> sometimes...

ex<u>claim</u>   ex<u>clam</u>ation

These words are still from the <u>same family</u> — the root is just <u>spelled differently</u>.

Word Families Have Similar Meanings

1) Words that are from the same <u>word family</u> are <u>about the same topic</u> or thing.

a<u>long</u>   head<u>long</u>   ob<u>long</u>

These words are all to do with going <u>in a straight line</u>.

2) If you <u>can't tell</u> what the <u>root</u> means straight away, you can work it out from the <u>meaning of the words</u>.

<u>frac</u>tion   <u>frag</u>ment   <u>frac</u>ture

These words are all about things that are <u>broken</u>, so you can guess that's what the <u>root</u> means.

EXAMPLE: What does the root '<u>anim</u>' mean in this word family?

animate   animation   animal   animator

creature ☐   cartoon ☐

puppet ☐   life ☑

The root 'anim' means <u>life</u>. Each word is to do with being or seeming <u>alive</u>.

"I can tell which words are from the same family and work out what roots mean."

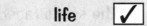

Synonyms and Antonyms

Synonyms Mean the Same Thing

A synonym is a word that has the same or a very similar meaning to another word.

The baby elephant is very heavy.

hefty   weighty

These synonyms could replace the word 'heavy' and the sentence would have the same meaning.

EXAMPLE: Tick one word which is a synonym of 'colossal'.

tiny ☐   enormous ✓   amazing ☐   imaginary ☐

'Enormous' means the same as 'colossal'.

Antonyms are Opposites

An antonym is a word that means the opposite of another word.

The car stopped suddenly.

slowly   gradually   gently

These antonyms have the opposite meaning to suddenly.

EXAMPLE: Underline the two words that are antonyms of each other.

The problem is I'm a very clumsy person. You need to be graceful to be a waiter, which is why I'm bad at it.

'Clumsy' and 'graceful' are opposites.

"I know what synonyms and antonyms are and can come up with my own."

Practice Questions

1   Put a different **prefix** at the start of each word below to make a **new word**.

.... happy   .... behave   .... star

2   Circle **two suffixes** which can be added to the word below to create new words.

equal

er   ity   ly   ate   ify

3   Look at the **word family** below.
What does the root '**act**' mean in this word family?

action   active   react   inactivity

Tick **one** box.

play ☐   do ☐   reply ☐   game ☐

4   Read the sentence below.
Circle the two words that are **synonyms** of each other.

Mia is brave to go on that scary ride — I'll never be that courageous.

5   Draw a line to match each word with its **antonym**.
You can only use each antonym **once**.

Word	Antonym
hide	humble
help	reveal
despair	hinder
arrogant	hope

Plurals

Add an 's' to Make Most Things Plural

With most words, just add an 's' to make them plural:

jumper → jumpers

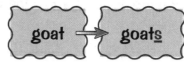
goat → goats

Some Plurals Are a Little Different...

1) Add 'es' to words that end in 'ch', 'sh', 's', 'x' and 'z'.

sandwich → sandwiches   box → boxes

2) Some words ending in 'o' have an 's' at the end when plural, while others have 'es'.

kangaroo → kangaroos   potato → potatoes

3) There are two options for words ending in 'y'.
If the letter before the 'y' is a vowel, just add an 's':

monkey → monkeys

4) But if the letter before the 'y' is a consonant, take off the 'y' and add 'ies':

butterfly → butterflies   baby → babies

Some Plurals Are Very Different...

1) Add 'ves' to some words ending in 'f' or 'fe'. Others just need an 's'.

leaf → leaves

knife → knives

roof → roofs

2) Some plural words are irregular.

child → children

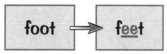
foot → feet

3) Some words stay the same in the plural:

deer   fish   sheep

"I can spell regular and irregular plurals."

Prefixes and Suffixes

Prefixes Add Letters to the Start of Words

1) The original word <u>never changes</u> when a <u>prefix</u> is added — just add the prefix to the <u>start</u> of the original word.

<u>re</u> + <u>turn</u> = <u>return</u>

prefix   word   new word

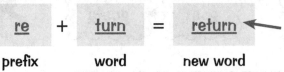
For more on prefixes and suffixes, see pages 50-51.

The original word is <u>spelled</u> the <u>same</u> after the <u>prefix</u> is added.

2) This means that sometimes you end up with a <u>double letter</u>:

i<u>rr</u>egular   mi<u>ss</u>pelled   i<u>mm</u>ature

Learn these Common Prefixes

It's important to know how to <u>spell</u> common <u>prefixes</u> and the <u>words</u> that <u>use</u> them...

SUB	<u>sub</u>heading <u>sub</u>marine	AUTO	<u>auto</u>pilot <u>auto</u>graph
INTER	<u>inter</u>national <u>inter</u>act	SUPER	<u>super</u>human <u>super</u>star
RE	<u>re</u>action <u>re</u>write	ANTI	<u>anti</u>septic <u>anti</u>social

Sometimes you can Add a Suffix Directly

Often you can <u>add</u> a suffix <u>without</u> having to <u>change</u> the original word.

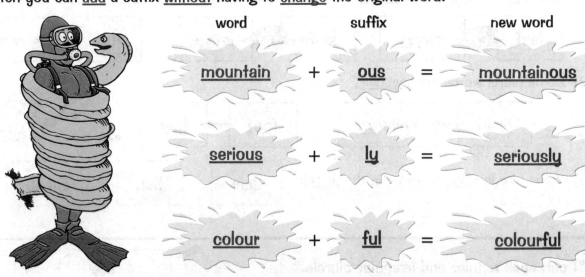

word   suffix   new word

<u>mountain</u> + <u>ous</u> = <u>mountainous</u>

<u>serious</u> + <u>ly</u> = <u>seriously</u>

<u>colour</u> + <u>ful</u> = <u>colourful</u>

Prefixes and Suffixes

Suffixes Sometimes Change Words

When a suffix is added, the word sometimes <u>changes</u>.

1) If the word ends in a <u>consonant</u> and a 'y', you normally <u>change</u> the 'y' to 'i'.

lonel<u>y</u>	+	<u>ness</u>	=	lonel<u>iness</u>
word		suffix		new word

2) When the word ends in '<u>e</u>' and the <u>first letter</u> of the <u>suffix</u> is a <u>vowel</u>, you lose the '<u>e</u>'.

adventur<u>e</u>	+	<u>ous</u>	=	adventur<u>ous</u>
word		suffix		new word

Sometimes You Need to Add a Double Letter

If the suffix starts with a <u>vowel</u> and the word ends with a <u>vowel</u> followed by a <u>consonant</u> (e.g. 'in') you need to <u>double the consonant</u> before adding the suffix.

word		suffix		new word
forg<u>et</u>	+	<u>ing</u>	=	forg<u>etting</u>
beg<u>in</u>	+	<u>er</u>	=	beg<u>inner</u>

> Say the words <u>out loud</u> — if you <u>emphasise</u> the <u>last syllable</u> it follows the <u>rule</u>. If you don't then it's an <u>exception</u>.

There are some <u>exceptions</u>, though:

gard<u>en</u>	+	<u>er</u>	=	gard<u>en</u>er		lim<u>it</u>	+	<u>ed</u>	=	lim<u>ited</u>

Look Out For Words Ending in 'cial' and 'tial'

At the end of words, a '<u>shul</u>' sound can be made by both '<u>cial</u>' and '<u>tial</u>'.
To find out which <u>ending</u> you should use, look at the <u>letter</u> that comes <u>before</u> it.

If it's a <u>vowel</u>, use 'cial'. ➝ off<u>icial</u>   sp<u>ecial</u>   artif<u>icial</u>

confide<u>ntial</u>   esse<u>ntial</u>   par<u>tial</u> ⬅ If it's a <u>consonant</u>, use 'tial'.

But there are <u>exceptions</u>:   financial   commercial   initial

---

"I can spell words that have prefixes and suffixes."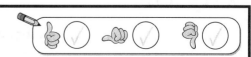

Homophones

Homophones Are Words that Sound the Same

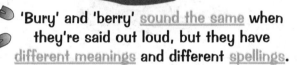

A homophone is a word that sounds the same as another word, but has a different meaning.

Where did you bury the treasure?

I'll have the berry yoghurt for dessert.

'Bury' and 'berry' sound the same when they're said out loud, but they have different meanings and different spellings.

Use the Sentence to Work Out the Word

1) To work out which homophone to use in a sentence, think about what the rest of the sentence means.

I flew the plain across the sea.   should be →   I flew the plane across the sea.

This doesn't make sense — 'plain' is the opposite of 'fancy'.

This sentence makes more sense — 'plane' is how you spell the word for the flying machine.

2) You can also work out which word to write down by thinking about the type of word that fits in the space.

Will the chillies affect the taste?

'Affect' is usually a verb. Remember: affect = action.

The chillies had an effect on the taste.

'Effect' is usually a noun.

The weather has been awful this summer.

'Weather' is a noun.

It doesn't matter whether it's sunny or not.

'Whether' is a conjunction.

"I can spell different homophones."

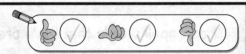

Silent Letters

Letters 'l', 'h', 'w' and 'b' Can be Silent

When a <u>letter</u> in a word isn't said <u>out loud</u>, it's called a '<u>silent letter</u>'.

1) There's sometimes a silent letter 'l' in the <u>middle of a word</u>.

| cou<u>l</u>d | wou<u>l</u>d | shou<u>l</u>d | ca<u>l</u>m | ha<u>l</u>f | ta<u>l</u>k |

2) '<u>H</u>' can be a silent letter too:

r<u>h</u>yme   w<u>h</u>at   g<u>h</u>ost

w<u>h</u>ale   r<u>h</u>ythm   w<u>h</u>en

3) There is often a silent 'w' <u>before an 'r'</u> at the start of a word.

<u>w</u>rong   <u>w</u>rapper   <u>w</u>rite

Look out for <u>other</u> silent 'w' words, like 'answer' and '<u>w</u>hole'.

4) There's sometimes a silent '<u>b</u>' <u>after 'm'</u> and <u>before 't'</u> at the <u>end</u> of words.

AFTER '<u>M</u>'

crum<u>b</u>   thum<u>b</u>   bom<u>b</u>   lam<u>b</u>

BEFORE '<u>T</u>'

de<u>b</u>t   dou<u>b</u>t

Silent 'g' and 'k' Sometimes Come Before 'n'

Some words that <u>sound like</u> they start with '<u>n</u>' actually have a <u>silent letter</u> at the start.

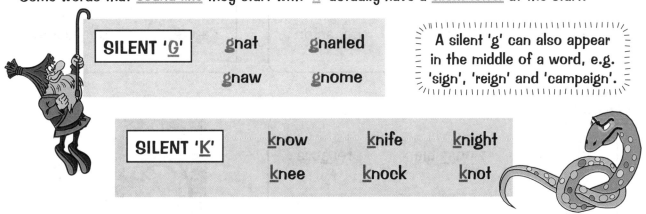

SILENT '<u>G</u>'   <u>g</u>nat   <u>g</u>narled   <u>g</u>naw   <u>g</u>nome

A silent 'g' can also appear in the middle of a word, e.g. 'sign', 'reign' and 'campaign'.

SILENT '<u>K</u>'   <u>k</u>now   <u>k</u>nife   <u>k</u>night   <u>k</u>nee   <u>k</u>nock   <u>k</u>not

"I can spell words with silent letters."

Spelling Tricky Words

Learn the 'i' Before 'e' Rule

Use this <u>rule</u> to decide whether 'i' comes <u>before</u> 'e' or <u>after</u> it:

> 'i' before 'e' except after 'c',
> but <u>only</u> when it rhymes with 'bee'.

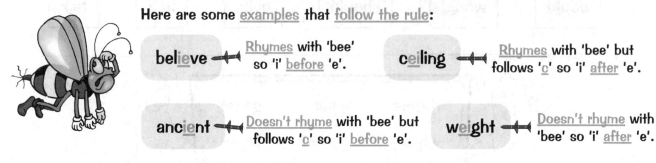

Here are some <u>examples</u> that <u>follow the rule</u>:

bel<u>ie</u>ve ← <u>Rhymes</u> with 'bee' so 'i' <u>before</u> 'e'.

c<u>ei</u>ling ← <u>Rhymes</u> with 'bee' but follows '<u>c</u>' so 'i' <u>after</u> 'e'.

anc<u>ie</u>nt ← <u>Doesn't rhyme</u> with 'bee' but follows '<u>c</u>' so 'i' <u>before</u> 'e'.

w<u>ei</u>ght ← <u>Doesn't rhyme</u> with 'bee' so 'i' <u>after</u> 'e'.

However, there are some <u>exceptions</u> you just have to learn.

prot<u>ei</u>n   s<u>ei</u>ze   caff<u>ei</u>ne ← In <u>these</u> words, the '<u>ie</u>' sound <u>rhymes</u> with 'bee' but the '<u>i</u>' comes after '<u>e</u>'.

boun<u>cie</u>st   fan<u>cie</u>d ← Some <u>suffixes</u> break the 'i' before 'e' rule.

Watch Out for Double Letters

<u>Double letters</u> in words can be tricky. <u>Learn these words</u> so you don't trip up in the test.

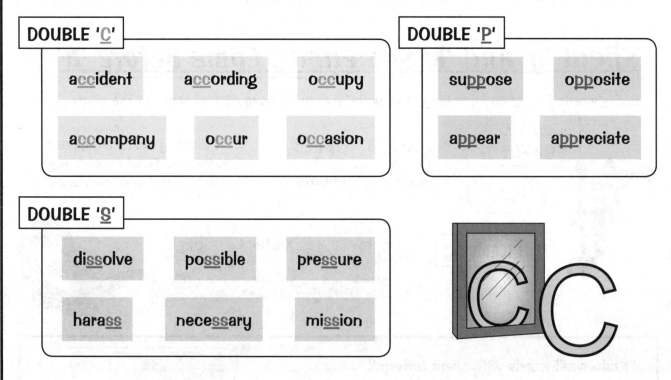

DOUBLE '<u>C</u>'

a<u>cc</u>ident   a<u>cc</u>ording   o<u>cc</u>upy

a<u>cc</u>ompany   o<u>cc</u>ur   o<u>cc</u>asion

DOUBLE '<u>P</u>'

su<u>pp</u>ose   o<u>pp</u>osite

a<u>pp</u>ear   a<u>pp</u>reciate

DOUBLE '<u>S</u>'

di<u>ss</u>olve   po<u>ss</u>ible   pre<u>ss</u>ure

hara<u>ss</u>   nece<u>ss</u>ary   mi<u>ss</u>ion

Spelling Tricky Words

'ough' Can Be Said in Different Ways

The '<u>ough</u>' group of letters can <u>sound very different</u> in <u>different words</u>. Start by <u>learning</u> these ones:

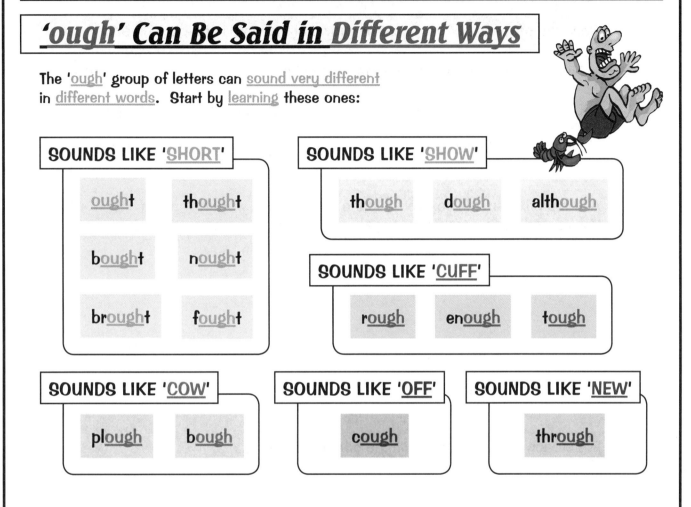

SOUNDS LIKE '<u>SHORT</u>'

<u>ough</u>t   th<u>ough</u>t

b<u>ough</u>t   n<u>ough</u>t

br<u>ough</u>t   f<u>ough</u>t

SOUNDS LIKE '<u>SHOW</u>'

th<u>ough</u>   d<u>ough</u>   alth<u>ough</u>

SOUNDS LIKE '<u>CUFF</u>'

r<u>ough</u>   en<u>ough</u>   t<u>ough</u>

SOUNDS LIKE '<u>COW</u>'

pl<u>ough</u>   b<u>ough</u>

SOUNDS LIKE '<u>OFF</u>'

c<u>ough</u>

SOUNDS LIKE '<u>NEW</u>'

thr<u>ough</u>

The Letters 'ch' Can Be Said in Different Ways

1) For <u>most 'ch' words</u>, the letters are pronounced like they are in the word '<u>ch</u>air':

<u>ch</u>eek   <u>ch</u>oose   mat<u>ch</u>   <u>Ch</u>ina

2) Some '<u>ch</u>' words <u>sound different</u>, so you need to listen out for them.

SOFT '<u>CH</u>'   ma<u>ch</u>ine   <u>ch</u>alet   <u>ch</u>ef ← The '<u>ch</u>' in these words is pronounced like the '<u>sh</u>' in <u>sh</u>oe.

HARD '<u>CH</u>'   s<u>ch</u>eme   stoma<u>ch</u>   <u>ch</u>emist ← In these words, the '<u>ch</u>' is pronounced like the '<u>k</u>' in <u>k</u>ite.

"I can spell tricky words."

Practice Questions

1   Read the passage below. Write the **plural** of the word in brackets in each space.

I went to the park with my grandad to feed the .... **[goose]**.

Later, we sat on one of the .... **[bench]** and had a picnic.

I then asked if I could throw some .... **[penny]** in the fountain.

2   Add a prefix from the box below to the start of each word to make a new word.
You can only use each prefix **once**.

sub	re	un

...................necessary

...................way

...................create

3   Write each of these words with the **correct spelling**.

confution ....

happyness ....

continueous ....

brightley ....

4   Draw lines to match each word to its meaning.

Meaning	Word
a set of two	pear
to slow down	pair
to destroy	break
a type of fruit	brake

Practice Questions

5   Look at the words below. For each word, write another
word that sounds the same but has a **different spelling**.

heal   ....

knead   ....

wait   ....

bear   ....

6   Look at the words below and tick the word that is spelt **correctly**.

Tick **one** box.

knoledge   ☐

knowledge   ☐

nowledge   ☐

gnowledge   ☐

7   Circle the word below that is spelt **incorrectly**.

resign   climb   stawk   whole   wreck

8   Read the sentences below. Circle the correct
word in brackets to complete each sentence.

Tamal was injured in a car **(accident / acident)**.

There isn't **(enugh / enough)** cake for all of us.

They're taking me up in a plane so I can try out my **(parashute / parachute)**.

9   The sentence below contains one spelling mistake. Circle the word
that is spelt incorrectly and write the correct spelling in the box.

Lindsay filled in the aplication form and posted it yesterday.

☐

Glossary

Adjective		A word that describes a noun, e.g. <u>fast</u> train, <u>tall</u> building.
Adverb		A word that describes a verb, e.g. shout <u>angrily</u>, walk <u>slowly</u>.
Adverbial		A word or group of words which acts like an adverb (it describes a verb), e.g. Angela walked the dog <u>in the afternoon</u>.
Antonym		A word that means the <u>opposite</u> of another word, e.g. <u>weak</u> and <u>strong</u>.
Apostrophe	'	Used to show <u>missing letters</u> and <u>belonging</u> (possession).
Article		The words '<u>the</u>', '<u>a</u>' or '<u>an</u>' which go before a noun. A type of <u>determiner</u>.
Brackets	( )	Used to separate <u>extra information</u> in a sentence.
Capital letter	A	Used for <u>proper nouns</u> and for <u>starting sentences</u>.
Clause		A bit of a sentence that contains <u>a verb</u> and someone <u>doing the action</u>.
Colon	:	Used to introduce some <u>lists</u> and to join <u>sentences</u>.
Comma	,	Separates items in a <u>list</u>, separates <u>extra information</u> and <u>joins clauses</u>.
Conjunction		A word or words used to <u>link</u> two <u>clauses</u> or <u>sentences</u>, e.g. <u>but</u>, <u>because</u>.
Contracted form		The <u>new word</u> made by <u>joining</u> two words together with an <u>apostrophe</u>.
Co-ordinating conjunction		A word that joins two <u>main clauses</u> in a sentence, e.g. <u>and</u>, <u>or</u>.
Dash	—	Used to separate <u>extra information</u> in a sentence.
Determiner		A word that goes before a <u>noun</u> to tell you whether it is <u>general</u> or <u>specific</u>.
Direct speech		The <u>actual</u> words that are <u>said</u> by someone.
Exclamation mark	!	Used to show strong <u>feelings</u> and for some <u>commands</u>.

Glossary

Full stop	.	Used to show where a sentence <u>ends</u>.
Homophones		Words that <u>sound the same</u> but have a <u>different meaning</u>, e.g. <u>by</u> and <u>buy</u>.
Inverted commas	" "	Used to show <u>direct speech</u>.
Main clause		An <u>important</u> bit of a sentence that would <u>make sense</u> on its own, e.g. <u>I ran</u> until my feet were sore. 'I ran' is the <u>main clause</u>.
Noun		A word that <u>names</u> something, e.g. <u>Jenny</u>, <u>computer</u>, <u>team</u>, <u>belief</u>.
Noun phrase		A group of words which includes a noun and any words that describe it, e.g. I drove past <u>the old music shop at the top of the hill</u>.
Phrase		A <u>small part</u> of a sentence, usually <u>without a verb</u>.
Prefix		<u>Letters</u> that can be put <u>in front</u> of a word to change its meaning, e.g. <u>un</u>tied.
Preposition		A word that tells you <u>how</u> things are <u>related</u>, e.g. <u>over</u>, <u>through</u>, <u>after</u>.
Pronoun		A word that can be used <u>instead of a noun</u>, e.g. <u>I</u>, <u>they</u>, <u>she</u>, <u>it</u>.
Question mark	?	Used at the end of <u>questions</u>.
Semi-colon	;	Used to separate <u>lists</u> of longer things and to <u>join</u> sentences.
Subordinate clause		A <u>less important</u> bit of a sentence which <u>doesn't make sense</u> on its own, e.g. <u>When it's cold</u>, I wear a hat. 'When it's cold' is the <u>subordinate clause</u>.
Subordinating conjunction		A word or group of words which joins a <u>main clause</u> to a subordinate clause, e.g. <u>although</u>, <u>until</u>.
Suffix		Letters that can be put <u>after</u> a word to change its meaning, e.g. point<u>less</u>.
Synonym		A word with <u>the same</u> or a <u>similar meaning</u> to another word, e.g. <u>yell</u> and <u>cry</u>.
Verb		A <u>doing</u> or <u>being</u> word, e.g. I <u>eat</u>, he <u>is</u>, they <u>know</u>.

Answers

Pages 10-19 — Section One: Reading

The Direction Dilemma

1) quickly

2) removed

3) It was faster.
   It was prettier.

4) They knew he wouldn't listen to them.

5) The path had carried them to high ground.

6) It was only lightly covering the peaks.

7) It was getting cold.

8) a) Richard, who stared blankly at the cafe, his mouth slightly open.

   b) He is very confident at first, but feels confused when they arrive back at the cafe.

9) He is arrogant and stubborn.

10) accusingly / snarled / snatching

11) As Beth says they've 'got a cold night ahead', they will sleep outside because they can't carry on walking in the dark.

The Marathon

1) The story might not be entirely true.

2) The Battle of Marathon

3) 26.2 miles

4) Windsor Castle

5) To raise money for charity, or to feel a sense of achievement.

6) annually

7) Over 6000

8) A run that is longer than a marathon.

9) The course passes through wild animals' habitats.

10) Because training can take up a lot of time.

11) Fact
    Fact
    Opinion
    Opinion

Something Told the Wild Geese

1) stirring

2) They could tell that cold weather was coming.

3) sagging

4) They remember the ice.

5) cautioned / stiffened

6) summer sun

7) Geese know to leave before winter arrives.

Pages 27-28 — Section Two: Word Types

1) Example of using offer as a noun:
   Amelia made an **offer** for the teapot.
   Example of using offer as a verb:
   The shop owner might **offer** Amelia a discount.

   In the first part of the answer, the offer needs to be a thing. In the second part of the answer, someone in the sentence needs to be doing the offering.

2) Omar **should** study for the test, but he **might** go to the cinema instead.

3) Patrick and Carmen were clever, but they were **lazy**.

   Many adjectives are acceptable here.

4) Sebastian went on holiday with his family to a **beautiful** part of the countryside. They rented a house in an area that was **hilly**, but close to the local village. They had a very **peaceful** holiday.

5) Adverb
   Adjective
   Adverb

6) Shirley must run **quickly** to the station because the train leaves **soon**.

   Don't miss adverbs of time, like 'soon.'

7) Fatima heard a strange noise and hid **under** the bed. She stayed there **until** four o'clock. When she eventually looked **through** the window, she saw a strange, dark shape moving towards her.

8) I liked the old clock, so the woman gave **it** to me for free.
   John loved the theatre, so **he** went to London to see a musical.

9) My family and our neighbours each own a bouncy castle. **We** keep ours inside, but **theirs** is so big that it has to stay outside.

10) **The** cabbages look great, but we need **a** leek to complete **the** recipe.

Pages 38-39 — Section Three: Sentences and Tenses

1) Ewen has an expensive camera — **statement**
   What a scary robot that is — **exclamation**
   Put your rubbish in the bin — **command**
   Do you have a pet guinea pig — **question**

2) Later that day, **Marie** decided to play football.
   Despite the hot weather, **he** was wearing a woolly jumper.
   Pancakes are delicious with some maple syrup.

Answers

3) a subordinate clause

'The trees shook violently in the wind' is the main clause of the sentence, so 'while we watched from the window' is the subordinate clause.

4) **While** Eliza was away, Mario sneaked into her room to play with her toys. He put everything back, **but** Eliza still knew.

5) The choir sang the songs beautifully.

6) The teacher told the children to stop talking.

7) After school, I **did** my homework then **played** my violin.

8) E.g. furious

Any word that has a similar meaning to 'fuming' but is more formal is acceptable here.

9) Oliver looked at his notes during the test and the teacher **saw** him.
Cherie ties her shoes **weirdly**.
Hassan had not seen **anybody** in the park all evening.

Pages 48-49 — Section Four: Punctuation

1) **mary seacole** was a nurse from **jamaica**. **she** was born in 1805 and died in **england** on the 14th of **may** 1881.

2) question mark

3) The athlete was fast**,** strong and very determined.

4) As soon as he could, Mr Andrews called the fire brigade.

5) We'll meet at the **gardener's** hut on the east side of the park. I've heard that it is always nice and quiet there, and we've got loads of time to walk.

6) "It's been raining all day here," said Gabby.

7) incorrectly
correctly
correctly
correctly

8) Lots of television crews went to the shore**;** they were all hoping to film the monster that lived in the water.

9) The mechanic (who came from the neighbouring village) started working on Jeffrey's car.

10) There's a mouse-eating rabbit in the garden.

Page 54 — Section Five: Vocabulary

1) **un**happy
misbehave
superstar

2) ity, ly

Using these two suffixes, you can make the words 'equality' and 'equally'.

3) do

4) Mia is **brave** to go on that scary ride — I'll never be that **courageous**.

5) hide — **reveal**
help — **hinder**
despair — **hope**
arrogant — **humble**

Pages 62-63 — Section Six: Spelling

1) I went to the park with my grandad to feed the **geese**.
Later, we sat on one of the **benches** and had a picnic.
I then asked if I could throw some **pennies** in the fountain.

2) **un**necessary
subway
recreate

3) confusion
happiness
continuous
brightly

4) a set of two — **pair**
to slow down — **brake**
to destroy — **break**
a type of fruit — **pear**

5) heel
need
weight
bare

6) knowledge

7) stawk

It should be 'stalk' or 'stork'.

8) Tamal was injured in a car **accident**.
There isn't **enough** cake for all of us.
They're taking me up in a plane so I can try out my **parachute**.

9) **aplication** should be spelled **application**.

Index

E6FR21